I Like Weather!

How Does the Sun Make Weather?

Judith Williams

Enslow Elementary
an imprint of
Enslow Publishers, Inc.

E

40 Industrial Road   PO Box 38
Box 398   Aldershot
Berkeley Heights, NJ 07922 Hants GU12 6BP
USA   UK

http://www.enslow.com

Words to Know

cycle (SY cuhl)—A group of things that happen over and over in the same order.

drought (DROUT)—A long time with little or no rain.

UV index—A chart to show how strong the sun's rays are each day.

water vapor (WAH tur VAY pur)—Water that has turned into a gas, such as steam.

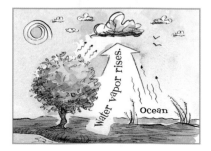

Contents

Where does weather start? 4

Where does the water vapor go? 8

What happens next? 9

The Water Cycle 10

Why is the weather warmer
in the summer? 12

How strong are the sun's rays today? 14

Is there a safe way to look at the sun? 16

Can the weather be too hot? 18

Experiment 20

Learn More
  Books 22
  Web Sites 23

Index 24

Where does weather start?

Earth's weather begins in outer space.
That is because the sun is a star.

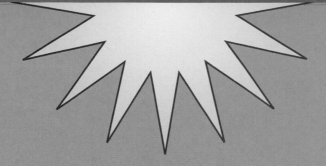

When the sun shines on Earth, it brings light and heat to our world. Heat is where weather starts!

The sun heats the earth. Water in the air, soil, plants, rivers, and oceans gets warmer.

When water heats up, it turns into water vapor. You cannot see it. When water vapor cools, you *can* see it. It is fog.

Where does the water vapor go?

It goes up! It rises into the sky.

The higher it goes, the colder it gets.
The cooled water vapor forms clouds.

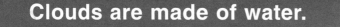

Clouds are made of water.

What happens next?

Rain falls from the clouds. When the sun shines again, the cycle begins all over!

The Water Cycle

Clouds

Rain

Water falls from clouds as rain. The sun heats the earth and water vapor rises to make clouds. This is called the water cycle.

Why is the weather warmer in the summer?

In the summer, we get more sunlight. This makes it hotter.

In the winter, we get less sunlight. This makes it colder.

How does this happen?

Earth is tilted as it goes around the sun.

North America is tilted *toward* the sun in the summer.

North America is tilted *away* from the sun in the winter.

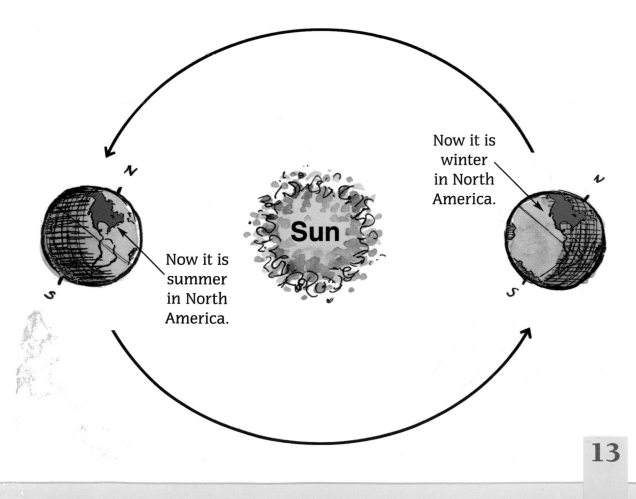

Now it is summer in North America.

Now it is winter in North America.

Sun

How strong are the sun's rays today?

The UV index is a chart that tells you. A high number means your skin can sunburn quickly.

UV Index	
UV Index Number	**How high is the danger of sunburn?**
0 to 2	Low
3 to 5	Medium
6 to 7	High
8 to 10	Very high
11 and higher	Extreme

sunscreen

Wear sunglasses, a hat, and clothes that cover your skin. Always use sunscreen.

Is there a safe way to look at the sun?

No! Even with sunglasses, it is not safe. Instead, look for your shadow.

A short shadow—or none at all—means the sun is overhead. This is the time of day when the sun's rays are strongest. Move into the shade or go inside.

You can only see your shadow on a sunny day.

Can the weather be too hot?

Yes. If the weather is hot for a long time, it is called a heat wave.

Weeks, months, or years with little or no rain can cause a drought.

This lake is almost empty because of a drought.

18

In a drought, drinking water dries up and crops do not grow.

19

How can you find out if there is water in plants and soil?

You will need:

- ❖ small plant
- ❖ sunny window
- ❖ clear plastic bag

1. On a sunny day, put a small plant in a sunny window in the morning. Cover the plant carefully with a large, clear plastic bag.

2. Late in the day, look at the bag again. Do you see any water drops inside the bag? Where did the water come from?

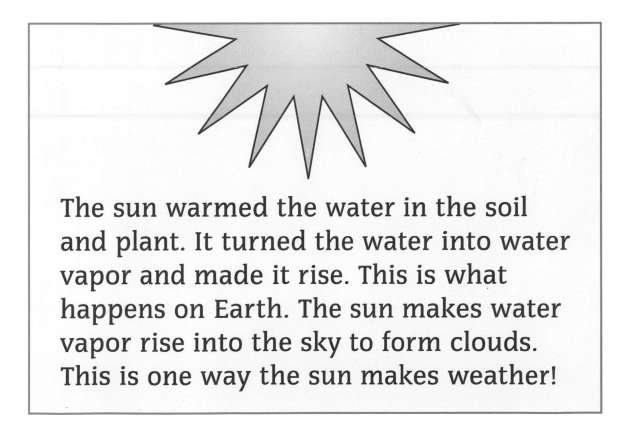

The sun warmed the water in the soil and plant. It turned the water into water vapor and made it rise. This is what happens on Earth. The sun makes water vapor rise into the sky to form clouds. This is one way the sun makes weather!

Learn More

Books

Ashwell, Miranda, and Andy Owen. *Sunshine*. Des Plaines, Ill.: Heinemann Library, 1999.

Fowler, Allan. *Energy from the Sun*. Danbury, Conn.: Children's Press, 1997.

Tomecek, Steve. *Sun*. Washington, D.C.: National Geographic Society, 2001.

Web Sites

U.S. Environmental Protection Agency.
Daily UV Index Map.
http://www.epa.gov/sunwise/uvindexcontour.html

NOAA, National Weather Service. *Playtime for Kids*.
http://www.nws.noaa.gov/om/reachout/kidspage.shtml

Index

clouds, 8, 11
cycle, 9, 10–11
drought, 18
Earth, 4, 13
fog, 7
heat, 5, 6
heat wave, 18
light, 5

outer space, 4
rain, 9, 11
shadow, 16
star, 4
steam, 7
summer, 12–13
sun, 4, 5, 9, 12, 13, 14, 16
sunburn, 14

sun rays, 14, 16
sunscreen, 15
UV index, 14
water, 6
water cycle, 10–11
water vapor, 7, 8, 11
weather, 4, 12, 18

Enslow Elementary, an imprint of Enslow Publishers, Inc.

Enslow Elementary® is a registered trademark of Enslow Publishers, Inc.

Copyright © 2005 by Enslow Publishers, Inc.

All rights reserved.

No part of this book may be reproduced by any means without the written permission of the publisher.

Library of Congress Cataloging-in-Publication Data

Williams, Judith (Judith A.)
   How does the sun make weather? / Judy Horan.
      p. cm. – (I like weather!)
   Includes bibliographical references and index.
   ISBN 0-7660-2317-6 (hardcover)
   1. Weather—Juvenile literature. I. Title. II. Series.
      QC981.3.W548 2005
      551.6-dc22

                                    2004012153

Printed in the United States of America

10 9 8 7 6 5 4 3 2

To Our Readers: We have done our best to make sure all Internet Addresses in this book were active and appropriate when we went to press. However, the author and the publisher have no control over and assume no liability for the material available on those Internet sites or on other Web sites they may link to. Any comments or suggestions can be sent by e-mail to comments@enslow.com or to the address on the back cover.

Photo Credits: © 2004 age fotostock, p. 17; © Claudia Kunin/CORBIS, p. 15 (background); © Copyright 1999–2004 Getty Images, Inc., p. 15 (background); © Corel Corporation, p. 2 ("UV index"); © Inga Spence/Visuals Unlimited, pp. 2 ("drought"), 19; © Luther Linkhart/ Visuals Unlimited, p. 18; © Mark Schneider/Visuals Unlimited, p. 8; © Miep van Damm/Masterfile, p. 12 (left); 2000 Copyright Photos forme.com, p. 15; Copyright © 1996–2004 JupiterImages, pp. 5, 6, 7, 9, 20 (left to right); Copyright © Wonderfile Corporation 2004, p. 12 (right); Enslow Publishers Inc., p. 4; Tom LaBaff, pp. 2 ("cycle" and "water vapor"), 10–11, 13.

Cover Photos: © Jeff Zaruba/CORBIS.

Every effort has been made to locate all copyright holders of material used in this book. If any errors or omissions have occurred, corrections will be made in future editions of this book.

Series Literacy Consultant	***Science Consultant***
Allan A. De Fina, Ph.D.	Harold Brooks, Ph.D.
Past President of the New Jersey	NOAA/National Severe
Reading Association	Storms Laboratory
Professor, Department of	Norman, Oklahoma
Literacy Education	
New Jersey City University	

Note to Parents and Teachers:
The **I Like Weather!** series supports the National Science Education Standards for K–4 science, including content standard CHANGES IN THE EARTH AND SKY. The Words to Know section introduces subject-specific vocabulary words, including pronunciation and definitions. Early readers may need help with these new words.